Flowers Without Rain

Flowers Without Rain

Electria Pullum

THE ECULLECTION

Cover Design: Electria Pullum
Illustration: Electria Pullum

ISBN: 9781791558178

No

Rain

No

Flowers

. . .

No

Purpose

No

Progress

My eyes are lost in the world,
But my ears are down for the night.
- Ad infinitum readers

Contents

Distorted

Lyrics.

. . . We all want to manifest new opportunities
but why are we afraid to *"Do It?"*

Note, I enjoy writing poems for a living . . . trying to figure out, "How can you be so **lost**?" Trying to understand yourself without being judge or being **slow** to your responsibilities.

 Therefore, I have **no tears left to cry** . . . although, I am still trying to figure out who am I, because personally; I don't know.

It's like giving up your dreams not your reality. I have **too** many emotions inside of me. I am **afraid** to send my messages to her.

Her as *me, myself* and *I*. Because she...is still growing.

LOST.

I am afraid of forgetting my old memories becoming a blur

When I see myself,

I see a mirror telling me to,

"THINK."

BLUR.

Thank you,

As the days had gotten older, the inflation of my sorrows had gotten higher

My heart became rich and famous, to be self-ware to water your expectations

Each day, what we shared, my love for you had gone unnoticed to receive an invitation

Unfaithfully, I pretended to have self-esteem

Now welcomes,

Pessimistic touch, hears, and sees

Optimistic unwanted rain

I feel light

I feel scarcity

I feel persistent

If I'm warm enough to be my own distraction

Pray for me

Please

Pray for me

Please

Pray!

DISTRACTION.

If your girl only knew

I was your one in a million

She wouldn't come over

I was extra smooth with my words

But, she couldn't read between the lines

Now, she's heartbroken

If you had only told her the truth

IF.

I wouldn't be this way,

If you love me the right way,

I knew something was in the way,

Cause your honesty wasn't here to stay,

You didn't even try to practice,

I was a ball, who was willing to play.

EXIT.

I desire my dreams to parallel my reality,

I want to right my wrongs,

So I don't hear paramedic screams,

So I will not have a thriller moment,

I'm just only hoping I perceive worthy needs,

I consider it.

CONSIDERATION.

Don't floss

Your identity away . . .

HALLUCINGOEN.

Hurt is past tense.

Hurtful is my present.

I wonder who I am, who am I

And understanding you're my choosey lover, mama

I cried angel tears for you I have suicidal thoughts

We don't know each other well

I came outta your vagina

We don't have a connection, when I got pushed out

I am a failure

Everything I am is an outsider to the world, mama

I want to dumb down . . . I don't know why

I can't answer your question because I know it will sound silly

But the day I turn 15, I can't hold your hand anymore

Even though, I don't think before I speak

But . . .

You have your own light

It's going to shine bright

I wish it very well for you

I can't even turn in the right direction

Pain.

Mother is past

Mom is present

Mama is the future

I hope you understand; I can't share it

I don't want any pain

Significantly,

A Young Child

P.S. I hope we meet again.

DESOLATION.

The night grew up

While the stars smile at me

I knew my dreams wasn't a fugitive

I finally found a hobby that is approachable

As I get closer to you

It is everything

I'm looking for?

RAPTURE.

Peace and quiet is all I need

Without it,

I'm not naturally free.

NATURAL.

Complexion skin

Endless pours

Fabricated opinions

Unwanted hatred

Too comfortable

For secondary rejections

Unconditionally,

~~Nobody is safe.~~

SAFE.

Will I fall?

Will I fly?

Addiction is the worst pain, you can get by

How else your organic soul can be reincarnated?

When your food for thought in debt with expenses

ORANGIC.

Love is a choosey lover

Not something divine and handpicked by God?

I feel my way out blind, as your fingers gaze my hip like the

curved edge of a saw – I'm full of dust -

I am still a foreigner in my body

If I peel enough layers, will I forget?

If I peel enough layers, will I get to eat my oranges?

Is my mind swollen and read like a narrative?

Waiting as I inhale, exhale

I raise my hand, I reach, if I could paint, it would be black

Black is intimidating, unfriendly and unapproachable

And also sexy, seductive, and intriguing

As I gaze at the wall

I stopped keeping track of time

Now I only think "here" and "there" is just a memory

 Later on, self- hatred became my identity

I unintentionally begin to change into the person that

compliments who I'm at that moment

Why did this happen to me?

If I give up my body

Do I get to go home?

I wish I were **Her,** Malcolm

I wish our love were Godspeed, made of stone

GODSPEED.

Ladies and gentlemen, you ask me to define who I am and I laugh at the silly question. I don't define me; everything else does. The art. The music. And the poetry. I lived by these three rebelling subjects. It became a trend to my childhood, later on, a tendency to my lifestyle. I never knew the path I can take with these three subjects and turn them into verbs. I hope in the future, the world (my audience) can be ecstatic and see me as a rock n roll adjective.

XXX.

Psychedelic
Addict.

*... Leave me **alone***

Whores are actions
Not appearances.

MARATHONS.

Can you hear the throb from my epic battles?

Can you see the listless walls haul my climax?

Never opening the doors for my needy cries

Never bestow tears to fight my colors that lies

Dull shadows deepen the weakness of my humanity

As guilt, hurt, and pain are triples messy words describing my lax

Wreck my boundaries for living and giving the ability to receive my own forgiveness

As my anxiety cries raucous my shame

Sorrow save my hunger

Cry my fear never ease my weary pain

Fear consume

Fear loves, fall, and die

I am fear, so how can I survive?

CRYBABY.

I choose to be by myself, once

Just once

Just at a time

Just for a moment

I messed up

When we fell in love, one time

We both became idealistic with our eyes

Our prototype proves to be manufactured

Our product is damaged

I just choose to be by myself, once

Just once

Just at a time

Just for a moment

I messed up

I knew you were my "practice", my "standby"

And realistic failure

PROTOTYPE.

Dear February,

I am afraid of love.

I am afraid of a simple touch, a feel, and a laugh.

My body cherishes the cold, I have no color.

I feel uncomfortable hearing your sweet melody.

I get goosebumps listening to you in the dark.

You keep me warm, just being yourself.

I am very thankful.

You make me feel, I'm at my best.

I wish my heart wasn't tainted so much.

I can easily forgive myself thinking, "Do I need love and affection?"

Only time can tell

Sincerely,

March

FEBRUARY.

Most of this text was written in the comfort of my bedroom, 'the floor of my domicile". This comfortable setting allowed me, the author time and space to think, analyze and critique, this social world we live in and do by. In doing so, I hope my poems serves as a catalyst and a beacon in many lives. **Note,** in writing these poems, my perspective stemmed from many realizations that goes on in life. This created many self-moments and a lot of writing. Also, I would like to give many thanks to my proud deserving "mother"! Your unwavering support and love will never be forgotten.

YELLOW.

Fences all around me

You whisper, " You love me."

My first response was, "Goodbye."

You scream, "NO!" later

You told me, you didn't want to reflect your own loneliness

However, I'm the process for you to move forward

Please compromise . . .

JUPITER.

Are you happy?

I'm just asking

I notice you never seem to smile

Can we walk and grab a cup of coffee?

You seem tense...

Am I hurting you?

I thought we were friends

I always wanted you

I'm the only one, who can hear you cry, too

You can't ignore me...

I'm everywhere, you can't escape me

I empty you

Do you still want your cup of coffee?

SOLITUDE.

I colored your soul,

Filling you up with pleasure and pain,

I whisper in your ear,

Screaming out your name,

And wrapping your hands around me,

Uhhh uhhh Uhhh

Na Na Na, honey

Just throbbing for your love

As we go deeper and deeper

And trust me,

You will lose your inhibitions

THROB.

If only time had stand still,

The luxury of sunlight,

Will have saved enough energy to heal

ULTRAVIOLET.

When the music goes off

The ears do too

PLUTO.

You don't feel like growing up

You can't see yourself living in your future

All you hear is complaining along the way

You're just waiting to give up

But some people feel like they know your life story

Hypocrites see smoking mirrors

As their cycle repeat

Complain yet to achieve

You feel like you owe them a baggage claim

You got to give them a reason for everything you do

You feel like your blonde moments are your collective thoughts

Do people really understand the meaning of self?

They give you answer but not a source

Their opinions

Their SPACE

You can't achieve without being a hypocrite

You got to learn value and order to enable logic

The mind walks; reasonable doubt talks

You can't tell me my SPACE

When your SPACE leans on ...

SPACE.

He tastes her,
With his fingers
She tastes him,
With her mouth

He loves to paint her,
Her body was a rock
He loves grip and hold,
He adores . . .

KANDY.

I know I'm ugly,

Nobody cares about me,

I want to keep it short and simple,

My flashbacks keep reminding me,

Who I live for,

Just leaves me crying,

You keep trying to explain,

Leaving me dancing in the night,

That's the only time,

I feel alive,

My question existing is reading between the lines

I hope I come out this battlefield alive,

Or else

TRAUMA.

I lost my sanity,

The day you died.

I realized . . .

You were just a term.

I was just too deep to understand,

You were a beautiful masterpiece with wise words.

It was so hard to comprehend,

I thought about killing you.

You was the victim for my sins,

Raw, unpolished, and anointed.

I like being uninterested,

Its a blessing.

ANOINTED.

The idea of greatness

Is saying thank you

ZEALOUS

Soul

Glitch.

. . . Not a such thing

of wanting **more**

Who are you without feelings?

It's just a simple question. You can write all day to express your denial.

However, your anger, my anger can't relish our true feelings.

You see everything isn't black. You need white to understand the light.

Will I be fearful of my oppressor?

It's just a simple question. I don't have the answer to survive.

We are *LOST* in the world, although we continue to pray.

As I sit in silence wondering, if I can still be saved.

What is our destiny?

It's just a simple question. We stare back at each other trying to figure out, our own benefits.

As me and you read, sleep, listen, and eat with one of another.

We continue this borderline cycle.

I don't understand and neither do you.

Who are we without feelings?

A forbidden *FRUIT*

A thing that's desired all the more because it's not allowed

FRUIT.

I'm stuck.

My soul is on hold

My mind in redemption

My spirit became irresponsible

As I decorate my temple

I-

UNDECIDED

UNAPOLOGETIC

UNGRATEFUL

UNCONSCIOUS

UNTITLED

UN is cheaper to live

UN.

Her bones move in slow motion

As her eyes begin to dance

She's home alone now, drowning

She can't drink enough

What is left in her?

But, how can she?

You can't measure her scales

If her mind live in destruction

She died February 3rd

She was afraid to wake up.

SCALES.

As honey slip through my fingers

The sins cover my eyes

Being vulnerable empty my lies

I want to tell the world, I'm free

However, I only gave them a show

By the eye of contact

Is the art of letting go

HONEY.

And

When I am looking through the lens

I see everything

However, my eyes didn't capture anything

MALIBU.

Lord Knows...

Forever struggle in silence

Alone jaded in silence

Honesty dare in silence

Lord Knows...

Benediction pension save lives

Cherish souls have a price

Earn savor rights

Lord Knows…

Courage rave

Hail Mary revenge insanity waves

Testify a dark new age, blasphemy.

BLASPHEMY.

I believe in GOD,

I don't have a RELIGION.

- I have a problem when people use religion to oppress other

people

(Remember religion is MANKIND)

RELIGION.

He was really lovely trying to exceed your expectations

Your pendulum went higher and higher

He couldn't save enough for your love galore

He knows . . . he's not good enough

The insecurities are burning him inside

He realizes his endless thoughts are penny less

He ask?

How does it feel to have me thinking about you?

When you're not satisfied

Sorry to bother you, baby boy xoxo

PENDULUM.

I don't see color.

- LOOK AT YOURSELF IN MIRROR, "BABY"

VAGUE.

Who said a man can give a woman everything she needs?

The Creator himself gave them lips, eyes, and eyebrows for their natural beauty,

However, they shave off their imperfections and draw their insecurities instead,

He gave them clarity, instead they were drinking remedy,

He gave them tough nails, so it won't break off; they clip it off,

He gave them a nose, chin, breasts, and a butt,

They resized it, duplicate it; for their own benefit,

If HE didn't satisfy them,

Who would think nasty men like us would please them?

NASTY.

A woman is a drug,

She's complicated like sugar and spice,

She respects - "No one is left behind"

She thrives ying and yang

She will leave a four-page letter and leave kisses

She is chanting when nobody is watching,

She's not a role,

She's pro-choice,

She's poison to society,

She let you come as you are,

She's not submissive of prejudice,

She's not a collective ideal,

She's - "ism"

She's not an idea; she's a structure,

She's a struggle,

She's a fighter

For womanism

WOMAN.

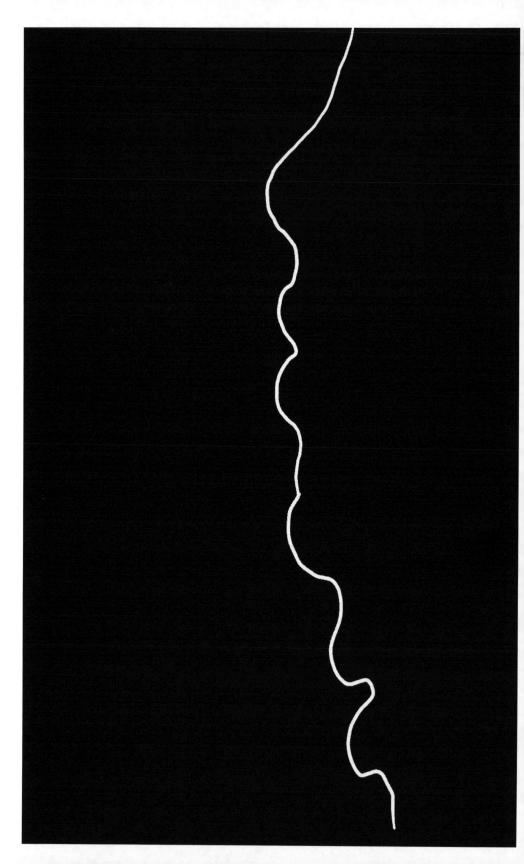

Three stages describing your good and bad habits,
If you can't please yourself,
Please don't play another role for somebody else.

IN TIME PROGRESS.

Flowers Without Rain is a journey about self- reflect. However, As the Arthur, I am speaking about feeling incomplete in my life and trying to find my past ambitions to help rekindle my personal goals. As I was writing this poetry book, I felt like my wavy journey is already falling apart in my life. In comparison to my childhood, which was stable and free. I'm lost in the complications of life itself. I may forget who I am, from the stress, angst, and agony. As when complications hit home harder than I can handle, I lose myself and I'm not as present as I would like or need to be. If my present self disappear, I manage to get by reflecting on the energetic of a child, still laughing within me. I wish, I could have the best of both worlds, when it comes to my youth. I just want to do better. I continue to look for answers from my past for advice.

DEFINE ME.

For my ad infinitum readers thank you for exploring this journey with me. Thank you for reading my poetry book, Flowers Without Rain.

AD INFINITUM READERS.

Electria Pullum is a current college student studying film and television, but has always had a desire for writing, whether it's poetry or putting together lyrics. To date, this is Electria's first book. Which is filled with healing, growth, and maturity. Electria shares her precious thoughts and dreams with her family. Before she started writing lyrics, Electria participated in many school activities and community outreach. If you want to know when Electria's next book will come out, or any event related to the "ECULLECTION"; please visit **thejourneyof2_** on Instagram or email **theEcullection@gmail.com**, where you can found out when she has her next release or an ECULLECTION event.

ABOUT ELECTRIA.